THE TEMPEST

SIMPLE SHAKESPEARE SERIES

JEANETTE VIGON

Copyright © 2023 Jeanette Vigon
All rights reserved.
ISBN: 9798322597483

This edition within the "Simple Shakespeare" series is a modern adaptation of William Shakespeare's "The Tempest," tailored for a broad audience by simplifying the language and reimagining scenes for contemporary understanding. While it preserves the core story and characters from Shakespeare's original, this version introduces significant modifications aimed at making the timeless tale accessible and engaging for modern readers. The adaptation respects the essence of the original work, offering a bridge between Shakespeare's Elizabethan English and today's vernacular, ensuring that the themes of love, conflict, and fate resonate with a 21st-century audience.

WHY I WROTE THIS BOOK THE WAY I DID

Crafting the "Simple Shakespeare" series was an endeavor fueled by a passion to make Shakespeare's timeless tales accessible and relatable to a modern audience, while retaining the essence that has captivated readers for centuries. The decision to reinterpret these classic plays in modern English and in a past tense novel style was rooted in the desire to bridge centuries of linguistic evolution, bringing the stories to life for contemporary readers who may find the original Early Modern English daunting.

The choice of a past tense novel format was a deliberate one, aimed at transforming the dynamic and immediate action of Shakespeare's plays into narratives that unfold with the thoughtful pace and introspection of a novel. This allows readers to immerse themselves deeply in the worlds Shakespeare created, experiencing the depth of character development and plot intricacies in a new light.

Translating Shakespeare's complex language and themes into modern English required careful consideration to preserve the nuanced storytelling and rich emotional tapestry of the original works. It was imperative to maintain the integrity of the stories, ensuring that the modernized versions stay true to the spirit of Shakespeare's intentions. This involved not only translating the language but also adapting the cultural and historical contexts to be more understandable, without diminishing the plays' original meanings and the universal themes they explore.

Furthermore, adapting these plays into a past tense narrative form necessitated a reimagining of Shakespeare's dramatic structure. The original acts and scenes, designed for the stage, were transformed into chapters and sections that flow seamlessly in written form, offering readers a cohesive and engaging narrative journey.

The "Simple Shakespeare" series is an homage to the enduring relevance of Shakespeare's work, crafted with the belief that the core of these stories—themes of love, power, fate, and human nature—are as resonant today as they were in Shakespeare's time. By presenting these tales in a form that is both familiar and fresh, the series aims to spark a new appreciation for Shakespeare among readers who might otherwise shy away from his work due to its original linguistic complexity.

In creating this series, it was my hope to demystify Shakespeare, proving that his plays are not relics of the past but living stories that continue to enlighten, entertain, and inspire. It has been a journey of discovery, not only in translating words but in unveiling the timeless humanity at the heart of Shakespeare's plays. I invite readers to explore these reimagined classics, to find joy in the stories that have shaped our literary heritage, and to see in them reflections of our own lives and times.

It has been a profound privilege to journey through the worlds of Shakespeare in this new light, and I am eager for readers to experience the magic of these stories, told anew.

INTRODUCTION

In this modern retelling of "The Tempest," William Shakespeare's profound narrative of magic, revenge, reconciliation, and love is vividly brought into the contemporary world, maintaining the enchanting essence of the original while situating it within a modern context that speaks to today's audience.

Set on a remote island that serves as the backdrop for an extraordinary convergence of the natural and the supernatural, the story transforms Prospero from a powerful sorcerer into a genius of our times, perhaps a reclusive inventor or a tech mogul, who manipulates the forces of nature and technology to bend the will of his visitors and orchestrate his grand design of vengeance and forgiveness.

Miranda and Ferdinand's tale of innocent love blossoms amidst a landscape of intrigue, as Prospero's machinations draw them together, illustrating the timeless nature of young love and its capacity to overcome adversity. The island itself, a character in its own right, might be envisioned as an unspoiled paradise at the edge of the world, representing the untamed beauty of nature and the potential for human intervention to both harness and disturb this balance.

Ariel and Caliban, embodying the spirit of rebellion and the yearning for freedom, are reimagined as beings caught between two worlds, their struggles reflecting the complex dynamics of power, servitude, and the desire for autonomy. Ariel could be seen as a manifestation of the ethereal, perhaps a digital entity or an AI, highlighting themes of liberty and servitude in the digital age, while Caliban represents the indigenous and the marginalized, challenging the intruders with his raw, unyielding spirit.

This adaptation engages deeply with the themes of power and its abuse, the redemptive power of forgiveness, the complexity of human relationships, and the eternal conflict between civilization and nature. By translating Shakespeare's eloquent prose into the modern vernacular, this version renders the narrative accessible and compelling, ensuring that the profound emotional depth and the philosophical underpinnings of the original text resonate with a contemporary audience.

Emphasizing the visual and emotional aspects of the story, this modern version of "The Tempest" offers a rich and dynamic exploration of the human condition, inviting the audience to ponder the intricacies of human nature, the transformative power of love and forgiveness, and the indelible impact of our actions on the world around us.

As the drama unfolds on this isolated island, transformed into a microcosm of human society, the timeless inquiries into freedom, justice, and the essence of humanity speak to modern viewers with renewed urgency and relevance. This adaptation invites us to immerse ourselves in the magic of Shakespeare's final masterpiece, demonstrating that his profound insights into the heart and soul of mankind remain as poignant and captivating today as they were over four centuries ago.

ACT I

SCENE 1

The ship was caught in a fierce storm, with thunder rolling and lightning flashing across the sky. The captain shouted for the boatswain.

"Boatswain!"

"Right here, captain. What's going on?"

"Get the crew moving quickly, or we're going to crash. Hurry, hurry!"

. . .

As the captain left, the boatswain turned to the mariners rushing in.

"Come on, everyone! Let's move, move! Get that sail down. Listen for my whistle and work as if your life depends on it!"

Suddenly, Alonso, Sebastian, Antonio, Ferdinand, Gonzalo, and others from the nobility stumbled onto the deck.

Alonso, the king, shouted over the storm, "Boatswain, be careful! Where's the captain? We need to act like men here."

The boatswain, barely looking up, responded, "Please, stay below deck."

Antonio, curious and concerned, asked, "Where's the captain, boatswain?"

. . .

"Can't you hear him giving orders? Your being here only makes things harder. Stay in your cabins; you're making the storm worse."

Gonzalo tried to calm the situation, "Let's be patient."

The boatswain snapped back, "I'll be patient when the sea is calm. Out of my way! Do you think the storm cares about your titles? Get back inside, and don't bother us."

Gonzalo, attempting to remind the boatswain of their rank and the respect due, said, "Remember who else is on this ship with you."

Their words were almost drowned out by the sound of the raging storm, as everyone struggled to find safety and manage their duties amidst the chaos.

. . .

The boatswain, frustrated and focused, had little patience for the nobles' complaints. "I don't care for anyone more than I care for myself. You're a counselor; if you can command this storm to calm down, then we'll stop working. If you can't, then be thankful you've lived this long and prepare for the worst in your cabin. Now, out of my way!"

With that, he left, and Gonzalo mused to himself, "I actually find comfort in his attitude. He doesn't look like someone who'd drown; he's more likely to hang. Let's hope fate keeps him alive for that. If he's not meant to hang, we're in deep trouble."

After a brief moment, the boatswain re-entered, shouting orders to manage the ship's sails amid cries of panic.

"This yelling is worse than the storm itself!"

Sebastian, Antonio, and Gonzalo reappeared, unable to stay away.

. . .

"What are you doing back here? Do you want us to just give up and sink?"

Sebastian lashed out, "Curse you, you noisy, godless brute!"

The boatswain retorted, "Then get to work."

Antonio added his own insult, "Die, you dog, you noisy fool! We're not scared of drowning like you are."

Gonzalo, trying to lighten the mood, joked, "He's safe from drowning, even if this ship is as fragile as a shell and leaking like a sieve."

The boatswain, amidst the chaos, tried to steer the ship away from danger. "Turn her away from the wind, set her back to sea!"

. . .

Mariners, soaked to the bone, stumbled onto the deck, despairing. "It's all over! Pray, everyone, pray! We're doomed!"

"Are we giving up already?" the boatswain shouted back, refusing to lose hope.

Gonzalo, with a sense of solidarity, said, "The king and the prince are praying. Let's join them. Our fate is tied to theirs."

Sebastian was losing his temper, "This is unbearable."

Antonio bitterly remarked, "Our lives are being thrown away by a bunch of drunkards. I wish this fool would drown in the sea he's so fond of!"

. . .

Gonzalo, however, held onto a sliver of hope, "He might yet survive, even if the sea itself tried to swallow him whole."

The air was filled with cries of despair, "Mercy on us!" "We're going down!" "Goodbye, my family!" "Goodbye, brother!" "We're lost!"

Antonio then suggested, "Let's die with the king."

Sebastian agreed, "Yes, let's bid him farewell."

As they left, Gonzalo reflected on his wish for solid ground over the treacherous sea, "I'd trade all this sea for just a piece of dry land, no matter how barren. Let fate do as it will; I'd much rather die on land than at sea." With that, he too exited the chaotic scene.

SCENE 2

Prospero and Miranda stepped out before Prospero's dwelling, the air still holding the smell of the recent tempest.

Miranda, visibly upset by the chaos she witnessed, turned to her father, her voice filled with concern. "Father, was it your magic that caused this terrible storm? Please, make it stop. The heavens seemed angry, ready to spill fires upon us, if the sea hadn't quenched them. I felt every pain of those suffering on that ship that broke apart. Their cries pierced my heart. If I had any power, I would have buried the sea to save them."

. . .

Prospero, with a calming tone, urged her to gather herself. "Don't be so distressed. Believe me, no harm has been done."

"But how can you say that?" Miranda's voice trembled, tears welling in her eyes.

"No real harm," Prospero reassured, his voice gentle. "Everything I've done was for you, my dear. You, who knows so little about who you really are or where I come from. And you don't know yet that I'm far more than just Prospero, the man with a modest home here, and your father."

Miranda, puzzled, admitted, "I've never thought to question our life or your past."

"It's time you know more," Prospero said, a serious tone taking over. He extended his arm. "Help me take off this cloak." As he laid down his magical cloak, he continued, "Dry your eyes and take heart.

The shipwreck you saw and the cries you heard moved you deeply, I know. But with my magic, I made sure no one was hurt. Not a single person on that ship suffered more than a scare. Now, sit with me. There's much more you need to understand."

Miranda, with a hint of frustration, pointed out, "You've often started to tell me about my origins, but then you'd stop, leaving me hanging with more questions than answers."

"The time has come for you to know the whole story," Prospero declared, signaling the importance of the moment. "Can you remember anything from before we arrived here? I doubt it, since you were barely three years old at the time."

Miranda responded with a hint of surprise, "Actually, I do remember something. It's vague, like a dream, but I remember being cared for by four or five women."

. . .

"Yes, you had caretakers, and more," Prospero acknowledged, intrigued by her memory. "What else do you recall from that distant past? Anything before our life here might help you understand how we ended up on this island."

Miranda shook her head, "Nothing more, I'm afraid."

"Let me tell you then," Prospero began, taking a deep breath. "Twelve years ago, I was the Duke of Milan, a powerful man, and you, Miranda, were the princess, my heir."

Miranda, taken aback, questioned, "Aren't you my father?"

"Indeed, your mother was a woman of great virtue. She told me you were my daughter. As Duke of Milan, I was your father, and you were destined to inherit my title and position."

. . .

Miranda, now overwhelmed with emotion, exclaimed, "How did we end up here? Was it through some wrongdoing, or was it perhaps a blessing in disguise?"

Prospero confirmed Miranda's curiosity, "Yes, my child, it was both a wrongdoing that forced us from our home and a blessing that brought us here."

Miranda felt a pang of sorrow, "It pains me to think of the troubles I've caused you, troubles I don't even remember."

Prospero then began to unravel the past, "My brother, your uncle Antonio, is the one to blame. Despite my love for him, second only to you, he betrayed me. I entrusted him with the management of Milan, as I was engrossed in my studies, valuing knowledge and the arts above all else. My focus on learning made me a stranger to my own duties, and in my absence, Antonio seized power."

. . .

Miranda assured him of her attention, "I'm listening very carefully."

Prospero continued, "Antonio learned how to manipulate the political landscape, deciding who would rise and who would fall. He reshaped my administration, gaining control over both the people and the officials, turning my allies into his supporters. He became like ivy, wrapping around and draining the life from me, the tree."

Miranda, eager to show her understanding, responded, "I understand, sir."

Prospero implored Miranda to pay close attention. "In my dedication to study, neglecting the affairs of the state, I unwittingly nurtured my brother Antonio's darker side. My complete trust in him spawned a betrayal as profound as my trust was boundless. His authority, fueled not just by my wealth but by the power he could wield in my name, corrupted him. He convinced himself he was the rightful duke, adopting all the appearances and privileges of royalty, which only fueled his ambition further."

Miranda, moved by the story, assured him, "Your story is so compelling, it could make the deaf hear."

Prospero continued, "Antonio saw no difference between playing the role of duke and being one. He was so power-hungry that he allied with the King of Naples, agreeing to pay him tribute and swear fealty, thus subjugating Milan to Naples. This act of treachery was aimed not just at usurping my position but at erasing me and you from our rightful place."

Miranda exclaimed, "How terrible!"

"Consider his actions and their consequences," Prospero reflected. "Could such a man truly be considered a brother?"

. . .

Miranda, seeking to find some solace, remarked, "It's hard to believe that someone born of my grandmother could do such things. But history shows that even the best families can produce the worst individuals."

Prospero then detailed the coup, "The King of Naples, an old enemy of mine, was all too willing to support Antonio's scheme. They plotted to kill me and erase our lineage from Milan, offering the duchy to Antonio as a reward. Under cover of night, they launched their attack, forcibly removing us from our home, leaving behind everything I cared about, except for you, my crying child."

Miranda, deeply moved by the story, expressed her sorrow, "It's heartbreaking. I can't remember how I reacted then, but hearing this now brings tears to my eyes."

Prospero, seeing her reaction, encouraged her to listen a bit more, "Stay with me; there's more to this tale that leads us to our current situation. Without it, everything else might seem irrelevant."

Curious, Miranda asked, "Why didn't they kill us when they had the chance?"

Prospero nodded at the question, "Good question. They didn't dare, thanks to the love my people had for me. They couldn't mar their scheme with such an overt act of violence. Instead, they put us on a ship, then transferred us to a dilapidated boat that was so unfit for the sea that even the rats had abandoned it. They left us there, adrift, to call for help to a sea that couldn't hear and to winds that could only offer their own kind of sorrowful response."

Miranda, reflecting on the hardship, wondered, "What a burden I must have been to you then!"

"No, my child," Prospero assured her with a fond smile. "You were like an angel to me, your smile gave me strength. It was as if courage from the heavens infused my spirit, helping me to bear our fate with resilience."

"How did we survive?" Miranda asked, intrigued by their miraculous survival.

"It was divine providence," Prospero explained. "We had some food and fresh water, thanks to the kindness of Gonzalo, a nobleman from Naples who was in charge of our exile. He secretly provided us with supplies, clothes, and other essentials. Out of his kindness and knowing my love for books, he also saved some volumes from my library, which have been invaluable to me. Those books, Miranda, are treasures I value more than my lost dukedom."

Miranda, touched by the tale of their benefactor, expressed a wish to meet Gonzalo, "I hope I get the chance to meet this kind man someday."

. . .

Prospero, acknowledging her wish, stood up, reclaiming his mantle, "Let's focus now. As we settled on this island, I've been your teacher, providing you with an education that many princesses, despite their leisure and tutors, might not match."

Miranda, filled with gratitude, thanked the heavens for Prospero's care. Yet, her curiosity about the storm couldn't be quelled, "But why, sir, did you create this storm?"

Prospero began to reveal his intentions, "Fate has played a hand in bringing my foes to this island. My abilities tell me that this moment is crucial for our future. If I don't act now, we might lose this opportunity for good. But let's pause on the questions—you seem tired, and it's natural to feel so after such revelations."

As Miranda drifted into sleep, Prospero called out for his spirit servant, Ariel, ready to move forward with his plans.

. . .

Ariel appeared with enthusiasm, ready to serve, "I'm here, master, ready to do whatever you need—fly, swim, dive, or ride the clouds."

Prospero, eager to know the outcome of his orders, asked, "Did you complete the storm as I directed?"

Ariel detailed the execution of the storm with precision and flair, "I was everywhere on the king's ship—above, below, amidst the crew, igniting awe. I split myself into many, setting fire here and there, creating a spectacle no less startling than lightning before thunder, making even Neptune's waves shiver."

Prospero, impressed by Ariel's diligence, noted, "Such chaos would unsettle the strongest of minds."

Ariel confirmed, "Everyone was driven to madness by fear, resorting to desperate actions. The crew abandoned ship, while the prince, Ferdinand, his hair standing on end, was the first to leap overboard, exclaiming that hell was empty and all the devils were upon us."

"That's exactly what I wanted to hear!" Prospero exclaimed with a mix of pride and satisfaction, then asked, "But this all happened near the shore, right?"

"Yes, very close," Ariel assured.

Prospero, concerned for their safety, inquired, "And they are safe?"

Ariel reassured him, "Not a single person was harmed; their clothes are even fresher than before. And as you instructed, I've scattered them around the island. Ferdinand I've left isolated, sighing and sitting alone in a remote part of the island."

Prospero, turning his thoughts to the king's ship and the rest of the fleet, asked, "And what of the king's ship? How have you dealt with it and the rest of the fleet?"

Ariel reported, "The king's ship is safe in a hidden harbor, the same place where you once summoned me to collect dew. The crew is asleep below deck, charmed after their ordeal. The rest of the fleet, which I scattered, has regrouped and is now heading back to Naples, mourning their loss, believing the king perished with his ship."

Prospero acknowledged Ariel's work, "You've done exactly as I asked, but there's more to be done."

Ariel, aware of the passing time, asked, "What's the time now?"

"Afternoon," Prospero estimated, knowing they had to use their time wisely.

. . .

Ariel, feeling the weight of his tasks, reminded Prospero of a promise for freedom, "Isn't it time for my release?"

Prospero, taken aback, responded, "Are you asking for your freedom before the agreed time?"

Ariel pleaded, "Please remember the services I've faithfully provided, without deceit or error, and without complaint. You promised me an early release."

Prospero, challenging Ariel's impatience, reminded him of the torment from which he was rescued, "Do you forget the suffering I saved you from?"

Ariel admitted he hadn't forgotten, but Prospero pointed out, "You seem to think little of the tasks I've set for you, like navigating the deep sea or braving the cold northern winds. Remember, these tasks are part of our agreement."

. . .

Prospero, frustrated with Ariel's plea, accused him of forgetting the past, particularly the cruel witch Sycorax, who had ensnared Ariel long before Prospero's arrival. "Have you forgotten Sycorax, twisted with age and malice?"

Ariel assured him, "No, sir, I haven't."

Prospero, skeptical, pressed further about Sycorax's origins, "And where was she from?"

"Algiers," Ariel responded.

Prospero recounted Ariel's history to remind him, "Sycorax, notorious for her wicked deeds and sorceries, was exiled from Algiers. Despite her many crimes, her life was spared for one reason or another. Isn't that so?"

"Yes, sir," Ariel confirmed.

. . .

Prospero then detailed Ariel's torment under Sycorax's hand, "She was pregnant when she arrived here and left with her monstrous son after her death. You were her servant, too gentle to perform her vile commands. For your refusal, she imprisoned you in a split pine tree, where you suffered for twelve years until her death. Your cries of agony were trapped until I freed you."

Ariel acknowledged, mentioning Sycorax's son, Caliban.

Prospero continued, "Exactly, that Caliban, whom I now command. You know well the agony you were in; your howls could make wolves cry and bears grow restless. Sycorax couldn't undo the curse she placed on you, but it was my magic that freed you."

Ariel, humbled and understanding the severity of Prospero's threat, quickly offered his thanks and promised to do better. "Master, I'm grateful. I won't complain again."

. . .

Prospero, his tone still harsh, warned, "If you dare to grumble once more, I'll trap you in an oak tree to suffer for twelve winters."

Ariel, eager to avoid such a fate, assured Prospero of his loyalty and readiness to obey, "I beg your pardon, master. I'll follow your commands with a gentle spirit."

Satisfied with this promise, Prospero softened, offering a path to freedom, "Perform well, and in two days, you shall have your freedom."

Ariel, now overjoyed, responded eagerly, "What would you have me do, master?"

Prospero gave his next order, "Transform into a sea nymph, invisible to all but us. Go quickly and return in this guise."

. . .

As Ariel disappeared to fulfill his task, Prospero woke Miranda, who had been sleeping through their exchange. "Awake, dear heart. You've rested enough."

Miranda, groggy and disoriented, remarked, "Your story made me so heavy with sleep."

"We have work to do," Prospero gently prodded, "Let's visit Caliban, our sullen servant."

Miranda, displeased at the mention of Caliban, confessed, "I really don't like seeing him, sir."

Prospero nodded, "Yet we need him. He keeps our fire burning and does tasks we benefit from. Caliban! You there, respond!"

From somewhere unseen, Caliban's voice emerged, reluctant, "There's plenty of wood here already."

. . .

"Come out now! We have other tasks for you," Prospero demanded, just as Ariel, now a dazzling vision of a water-nymph, reappeared, ready for further instructions.

Ariel, committed to his task, quickly left to transform as ordered by Prospero.

Prospero then turned his attention to a less cooperative inhabitant of the island, Caliban, summoning him with a voice filled with disdain, "Come out, you offspring of evil, born from your wicked mother!"

Caliban emerged, cursing Prospero and Miranda with the bitterness of his words, "May the foulest of mists and winds blister and curse you both!"

Unmoved, Prospero retorted with a promise of punishment, "Tonight, you'll suffer cramps and pains, tormented by the spirits of the night, more intense than any sting of bees."

. . .

Caliban, undeterred, claimed his right to the island, inherited from his mother, Sycorax. He accused Prospero of usurping his land, recalling a time when Prospero treated him kindly, only to enslave him later, "This island was mine! You took it from me. You were kind at first, but now you imprison me, keeping the island's riches for yourself."

Prospero, angered, accused Caliban of ingratitude and betrayal, especially after attempting to harm his daughter, "You lie, and kindness does not move you. You tried to harm my child, and for that, you've lost any kindness I once showed."

Caliban, with a twisted sense of regret, wished his plan had succeeded, envisioning an island populated by his offspring, "If only you hadn't stopped me, this island would be filled with my own kind."

Prospero, with frustration and disdain, condemned Caliban's inability to embrace any shred of goodness despite being taught language and understanding, "You're capable of the worst, despite my efforts to educate you. Your nature is so vile that not even the most generous could tolerate you."

Caliban, bitter and resentful, saw his newfound ability to speak as a means to curse Prospero, "Your teaching only gave me the tools to curse you more effectively."

Prospero, unimpressed by Caliban's retort, ordered him to gather fuel, warning of severe punishments for any disobedience, "Fetch us fuel, and do it quickly. Resist or act lazily, and I'll torment you beyond your wildest fears."

Caliban, reluctantly agreeing, recognized the extent of Prospero's power, even fearing it could subdue the god worshipped by his mother, "I have no choice but to obey. His magic controls even the mightiest."

. . .

As Caliban left to carry out his tasks, Ariel reappeared, invisible, luring Ferdinand with a magical song that seemed to heal and guide him through his despair over his father's presumed death. Entranced by the melody, Ferdinand pondered whether the music was of the air or the earth, noting how it eased his sorrow and drew him forward, "Where is this divine music coming from? It calmed the storm's rage and my grief, leading me here." The music resumed, captivating him once more, hinting at the enchantment that Prospero and Ariel had woven around the island.

Ariel, invisible, let his voice float through the air, weaving a tale of transformation about Ferdinand's father, "Full fathom five thy father lies; of his bones are coral made; those are pearls that were his eyes: nothing of him that doth fade, but doth suffer a sea-change into something rich and strange."

Ferdinand, touched by the song, felt it spoke directly of his lost father. "This song, it's about my father, isn't it? This isn't something from this world. I can hear it all around me."

. . .

Prospero, watching closely, nudged Miranda, "Look there, through the trees. What do you see?"

Miranda, catching sight of Ferdinand, was immediately struck by his presence. "Is that a spirit? He's so... majestic. But it must be a spirit, right?"

Prospero explained, "No, he's a man, just like us. He's been through a lot, which mars his beauty somewhat, but if grief were absent, you'd find him very appealing. He's lost from his crew and wandering."

Miranda, enchanted, could hardly find the words. "He's like a god to me. I've never seen anything so noble in nature."

Prospero quietly reflected on the unfolding events, pleased with Ariel's work, "This is going exactly as I hoped. Ariel, for this, you'll have your freedom soon."

The Tempest

. . .

Ferdinand, noticing Miranda, mistook her for a celestial being, "Are you the divine being guiding me with that heavenly music? Please, tell me if you live here, and if you might offer me guidance. My deepest wish, which I'm almost afraid to ask, is to know—are you a maiden?"

Miranda, straightforward and innocent in her response, said, "There's no need for wonder; yes, I am a maiden."

Ferdinand, hearing his native tongue, was struck with wonder. "This language! I'd consider myself the most fluent speaker of it, if only I were where it's commonly spoken."

Prospero, intrigued, questioned him, "The best, you say? How would you fare if the King of Naples were to hear such a claim?"

. . .

Ferdinand, with a heavy heart, revealed his identity, "I am Naples. I saw with my own eyes—eyes that haven't stopped weeping since—the king, my father, perish in the sea."

Miranda, moved by his story, expressed her sorrow, "Oh, what a terrible fate!"

Ferdinand, revealing more of his tragedy, added, "Yes, and all his lords, the Duke of Milan and his brave son were with him."

Prospero, speaking aside, contemplated the power he and his courageous daughter held over Ferdinand and decided to promise Ariel his freedom for this development. To Ferdinand, he spoke more directly, suggesting he might be overstepping, "You might be misunderstanding your situation here."

Miranda, puzzled and distressed by her father's stern tone, thought to herself, "Why is he being so harsh? This is only the third man I've ever seen, but the first I've ever felt such a draw towards. I hope my father can be moved to favor him."

Ferdinand, captured by Miranda's presence, offered her a lofty position, "If you are a maiden and your heart is free, I would make you the Queen of Naples."

Prospero, interjecting firmly, "Hold there, young man. One more word. You're claiming titles and making promises as if you had rights here, accusing you of spying to usurp my domain."

Ferdinand, asserting his integrity, declared, "No, I am a man of honor."

Miranda, looking upon Ferdinand, argued that such a noble appearance could only house goodness. "A person as fair as he must harbor goodness within. Evil cannot prevail in such a place."

. . .

Prospero, unmoved by Miranda's pleas, commanded Ferdinand to follow him, threatening harsh treatment and confinement for his supposed treachery. "You'll be bound and fed on the barest of sustenance. Come with me."

Ferdinand, defiant, refused to submit to such treatment, asserting his strength until he found himself magically restrained, unable to move.

Miranda, distressed, implored her father to reconsider, praising Ferdinand's gentle nature. "Father, please, he's not a threat. He's brave, not prone to fear."

Prospero, asserting his authority, dismissed Ferdinand's defensive stance as mere posturing, warning him of his power to disarm and control him with magic. "Put away your sword. Your guilt betrays you, making you powerless against my magic."

. . .

Miranda, desperate, pleaded for her father's mercy, offering herself as a guarantee for Ferdinand's behavior.

Prospero, growing angry at Miranda's insistence, warned her against further intercession, criticizing her naivety and comparing Ferdinand unfavorably to Caliban, suggesting she sees Ferdinand as noble simply because she has seen no one else, save for Caliban. "Your judgment is clouded. To you, he may seem like an angel, but that's only because you know so little of the world and its people."

Miranda, with a gentle firmness, declared her contentment with Ferdinand, lacking any desire to find someone better. "I'm content with him; I have no wish to meet a more noble man."

Prospero, unmoved, urged obedience, remarking on Ferdinand's weakened state, as if his strength had reverted to that of a child. "Your body is as weak as if you were a newborn, without any strength."

. . .

Ferdinand, acknowledging this weakness, felt as though he was in a dream, constrained by invisible forces. Despite the loss of his father, the shipwreck, and Prospero's threats, the opportunity to see Miranda, even from the confines of a prison, seemed a liberty vast enough for him. "Everything I've endured is bearable if it means I can see her, even from captivity."

Prospero, aside, noted the effectiveness of his plan, acknowledging Ariel's role in the unfolding events. "This is going as planned. Well done, Ariel."

He then instructed Ferdinand to follow him while assigning Ariel another task with a promise of freedom for strict adherence to his commands. "Follow my commands to the letter, and you'll have your freedom."

Miranda tried to reassure Ferdinand, hinting at a gentler side of her father not visible in his current demeanor. "Don't worry; my father's usually kinder than this."

. . .

As they exited, Prospero's manipulation and control over the situation were evident, setting the stage for the trials and tests that would ultimately determine Ferdinand and Miranda's fate.

ACT II

SCENE 1

In a different part of the island, Alonso, Sebastian, Antonio, Gonzalo, Adrian, Francisco, and a few others were wandering when Gonzalo tried to lift the spirits of the group. "Please, sir, try to cheer up. We all have reasons to be happy. Our survival is a miracle far outweighing our loss. This kind of sorrow is not unique to us. Every day, some sailor's spouse, some business owner feels this kind of loss. But our miraculous survival is something not many can boast about. Think about it, weigh our losses against this incredible luck."

Alonso, tired and not in the mood for Gonzalo's optimism, simply responded, "Enough, please."

. . .

Sebastian, with a smirk, whispered to Antonio, "He takes comfort as eagerly as one would cold porridge."

Antonio chuckled, "He won't be easily cheered up, that's for sure."

Sebastian observed Gonzalo trying again and quipped, "Watch him go, winding up his wit. Any moment now, it'll go off."

Gonzalo tried to continue, "Sir—"

"One," Sebastian interrupted, "your point?"

Gonzalo, undeterred, went on, "When we welcome every piece of sorrow that's offered, it comes to dwell with us—"

. . .

"A dollar," Sebastian joked, implying that Gonzalo's words were cheap.

Gonzalo sighed, "You've actually made a truer point than you intended. Sorrow does indeed come to those who dwell on it."

"You've taken my jest more seriously than I meant," Sebastian replied, somewhat impressed.

Gonzalo attempted to continue, "Therefore, my lord—"

Antonio interjected, barely hiding his amusement, "My, what a waste of words he is!"

Alonso, feeling overwhelmed, pleaded, "I beg you, let's not continue this."

. . .

Gonzalo, sensing his words were not welcome, said, "Alright, I've said my piece, but—"

Sebastian, ever the cynic, couldn't help but comment, "He loves to talk."

Antonio, looking for amusement, suggested a bet to Sebastian, "Who do you think will start babbling first, he or Adrian?"

"The old one," Sebastian guessed.

"The young one," Antonio countered.

"Done," Sebastian agreed. "The bet is for a good laugh."

"A fair wager!" Antonio exclaimed.

. . .

Adrian, oblivious to their side conversation, remarked, "Despite its appearance of being deserted—"

Sebastian couldn't contain himself and laughed, "Ha, ha, ha! There, I win."

Adrian, trying to ignore him, continued, "It's hardly livable and nearly impossible to get to—"

"Yet," Sebastian interjected.

"Yet," Adrian persisted, determined to make his point.

Antonio teased, "He couldn't miss the chance to speak."

Adrian, focusing on his observation, said, "This place must have a very gentle, tender climate."

. . .

Antonio, playing with words, joked, "'Temperance' was quite the gentle lady."

Sebastian laughed, "Yes, and a cunning one, as he so scholarly pointed out."

Adrian, trying to stay on track, noted, "The air here is incredibly fresh."

Sebastian, with a smirk, added, "As if it had lungs, and diseased ones at that."

Antonio added, sarcastically, "Or as if it were scented by a swamp."

Gonzalo, ever the optimist, insisted, "This place has everything needed for life."

. . .

"True, except for a way to live," Antonio quipped.

"There's little or no means for that," Sebastian agreed.

Gonzalo, trying to find beauty in their surroundings, observed, "Look how lush and vibrant the grass is! How green!"

"The ground is more brown than green," Antonio corrected.

"With just a hint of green," Sebastian added, teasing Gonzalo's optimism.

"He's not far off," Antonio said, half-seriously.

"No, he's completely missing the truth," Sebastian countered with a laugh.

. . .

Gonzalo, trying to shift the conversation to something positive, mentioned, "But what's truly remarkable, almost unbelievably so—"

"As are many so-called wonders," Sebastian interrupted.

"—is that our clothes, despite being soaked in the sea, have kept their freshness and look as if they were newly dyed rather than salt-stained," Gonzalo continued.

"If his pockets could talk, wouldn't they accuse him of lying?" Antonio joked.

"Yes, or at least of embellishing the story quite generously," Sebastian joined in.

Gonzalo, not deterred, said, "I think our clothes seem as fresh as the day we wore them to the wedding of the king's daughter, Claribel, in Africa, when she married the King of Tunis."

"That was a beautiful wedding, and our journey back has been fortunate," Sebastian remarked, recalling the event fondly.

"Tunis has never been honored with such a queen before," Adrian added, praising the match and momentarily joining the conversation on a positive note.

Gonzalo nostalgically added, "Not since the time of widow Dido."

Antonio, unable to resist a jibe, exclaimed, "Widow! Curse that word! How did we end up talking about widow Dido?"

. . .

Sebastian, finding amusement in the reaction, teased, "Imagine if he mentioned 'widower Aeneas' too? You'd really have a fit then!"

Adrian, puzzled, joined in, "Widow Dido, you say? That's curious. She was from Carthage, not Tunis."

Gonzalo corrected him, "Actually, this place, Tunis, was once Carthage."

"Carthage?" Adrian echoed, surprised.

"Yes, I'm certain of it, Carthage," Gonzalo affirmed.

Sebastian, ever mocking, quipped, "His word's as powerful as a miraculous harp; he's rebuilt the city with just his speech."

Antonio wondered, "What next? What impossibility will he simplify for us?"

. . .

Sebastian speculated, "Perhaps he'll pocket this island and gift it to his son as if it were an apple."

"And by planting its seeds in the sea, he'd grow more islands," Antonio added, playing along.

"Yes," Gonzalo agreed, unfazed by their teasing.

"In due time," Antonio said, a hint of respect in his jest.

Gonzalo, trying to steer the conversation back, said, "We were discussing how our clothes seem as fresh as the day we were in Tunis for your daughter's wedding, now the queen."

"And the finest queen to ever grace the place," Antonio remarked, proud.

. . .

"Enough about widow Dido, please," Sebastian begged, although he couldn't help but repeat, "Oh, widow Dido! Yes, widow Dido."

Gonzalo, trying to lighten the mood, asked, "Isn't my jacket as fresh as the day I first wore it? I mean, more or less."

Antonio, ever the skeptic, replied, "That's a stretch, if ever there was one."

Gonzalo reminded him, "When I wore it at your daughter's wedding?"

Alonso, overwhelmed by their trivial conversation amidst his grief, burst out, "Your words are torture to me. I wish I had never agreed to my daughter's marriage in Tunis. Because of that decision, my son is lost, and my daughter is so far from Italy, I fear I'll never see her again. My heir to Naples and Milan, what cruel fate has claimed you?"

. . .

Francisco, trying to offer some hope, interjected, "Sir, there's a chance he may still be alive. I saw him fighting the waves, riding them with such strength. He was a master over the sea, making his way to the shore. I believe he could have made it to land alive."

Alonso, grief-stricken, could only respond, "No, he's gone."

Sebastian, blaming Alonso, said, "This loss is on you. You refused to marry your daughter in Europe, choosing instead to lose her to an African kingdom, far from your sight. You ignored our advice and the wishes of your own daughter, who was torn between her duty and her own desires. Now, we may have lost your son forever. Milan and Naples will mourn more for the widows this tragedy has created than for any comfort we can bring them. The blame is yours alone."

Alonso, unable to bear more, pleaded, "Please, no more."

. . .

Alonso, reflecting on their loss, murmured, "That's the hardest part to accept."

Gonzalo, addressing Sebastian's harsh words, advised, "Lord Sebastian, your truth could use a touch of kindness and better timing. You're aggravating the wound when you should be helping to heal it."

"Fair point," Sebastian conceded.

"And done with surgical precision," Antonio added wryly.

Gonzalo continued, "When you're in a foul mood, it casts a shadow over all of us."

"Foul weather, you say?" Sebastian questioned.

"Indeed, very foul," Antonio confirmed.

. . .

Gonzalo, lost in thought, mused, "If I had control over this island—"

"He'd probably plant it with nettles," Antonio interjected.

"Or thistles and weeds," Sebastian added, imagining a bleak scenario.

"But if I were its king, what would I do?" Gonzalo pondered aloud.

"You'd probably avoid getting drunk simply because there'd be no wine," Sebastian quipped.

"In my ideal commonwealth," Gonzalo elaborated, ignoring the jests, "everything would be opposite to our ways. There'd be no trade, no leaders, no literacy. Wealth and servitude wouldn't exist; no contracts, inheritance, boundaries, or private property; no farming, vineyards, or use of metals, grains, wine, or oil; no jobs. Everyone would be idle, men and women alike, living in innocence and purity, with no one ruling over others."

"And yet, you'd want to be its king," Sebastian pointed out the contradiction.

Antonio noted, "You seem to forget the end of your utopia as soon as you describe its beginning."

Gonzalo continued, dreaming of a utopia, "Everything nature produces would be shared, without the need for hard work or struggle. There'd be no crime, no weapons, no need for any tools of harm. Nature itself would provide abundantly for all, feeding my innocent people."

Sebastian, with a hint of mockery, asked, "And there would be no marriages among your people?"

. . .

"None at all," Antonio chimed in, "Everyone would be idle, living without rules."

Gonzalo, undeterred by their sarcasm, asserted, "I would govern so perfectly, it would surpass even the golden age."

"God save King Gonzalo!" Sebastian exclaimed in jest.

"Long may he reign!" Antonio declared, playing along.

Gonzalo, trying to make a point, said, "And, do you see what I'm getting at?"

Alonso, weary and uninterested, pleaded, "Please, no more. Your words mean nothing to me."

. . .

Gonzalo, understanding yet undeterred, responded, "I believe you, Your Highness. I only spoke to give these gentlemen a chance to exercise their wit, which they seem eager to use, laughing at the slightest provocation."

"It was you we laughed at," Antonio pointed out.

Gonzalo, unoffended, replied, "In this game of wit, I'm hardly a match for you, so you can carry on laughing at whatever pleases you."

"What a comeback!" Antonio exclaimed.

Sebastian added, "Though it fell a bit flat."

Gonzalo, with a gentle rebuke, said, "You're spirited fellows; you'd try to move the moon if you thought it stayed too long in its phase."

. . .

Just then, Ariel, unseen by all, entered, playing solemn music, adding a mysterious atmosphere to their conversation.

"We would indeed," Sebastian said, imagining the challenge, "And then perhaps go bird hunting at night."

Antonio, noticing Gonzalo's weariness, reassured him, "No need to be upset, my lord."

Gonzalo, tired but peaceful, replied, "I assure you, I won't be so foolish. Perhaps your laughter will lull me to sleep, as I'm feeling quite exhausted."

"Then sleep, and we'll be here," Antonio suggested.

As if on cue, everyone except Alonso, Sebastian, and Antonio succumbed to sleep. Alonso marveled at how quickly sleep took them, wishing his own troubling thoughts could be so easily stilled.

. . .

Sebastian encouraged him, "Don't pass up the chance to rest, sir. Sleep doesn't come easily to those burdened with sorrow, but when it does, it's a true solace."

"We'll stand guard and ensure your safety while you rest," Antonio offered, positioning themselves as loyal protectors.

Grateful, Alonso responded, "Thank you," and soon fell asleep under the heavy cloak of his own weariness.

Ariel, having silently observed and influenced the scene, left as quietly as he arrived.

Sebastian, puzzled by the sudden wave of sleepiness that overtook the others, remarked, "This is strange, how quickly they all fell asleep!"

. . .

"It must be the climate here," Antonio suggested, looking for a logical explanation.

"But why aren't we affected? I don't feel the slightest bit tired," Sebastian questioned, his curiosity piqued.

"Neither do I; my mind is too alert," Antonio agreed, sensing an opportunity. "It's as if they were struck down all at once. What could this mean for us, Sebastian? What opportunity does this present?" he hinted, with a glimmer of conspiracy in his voice.

Continuing, he hinted at ambition, "And yet, looking at you now, I can almost see it—your destiny. It's as if the situation itself and my own vivid imagination are placing a crown upon your head."

Sebastian, slightly bewildered, asked, "Are you awake?"

. . .

"Do you not hear me speaking to you?" Antonio replied, a hint of impatience in his voice.

"Yes, I hear you. But your words sound as if they're coming from someone half asleep. What were you saying? This is such an odd situation—to be asleep yet with eyes wide open, standing, talking, moving, and still so deeply asleep."

Antonio, seizing the moment to influence Sebastian, said, "Noble Sebastian, you're neglecting your chance at fortune—letting it die, even—while you're wide awake."

"You sound so clear, yet it's as if you're snoring. There's a purpose to your words," Sebastian observed, intrigued.

"I'm being more serious than usual," Antonio confessed. "You need to pay attention and take this seriously as well. It's important."

. . .

"I'm like stagnant water then," Sebastian remarked, indicating his readiness to be influenced.

"I can show you how to flow," Antonio offered, metaphorically suggesting he could guide Sebastian to action.

"Then teach me. I feel as though my own laziness is dragging me down," Sebastian admitted.

"Oh, if only you realized the potential of what you're dismissing with your jests! By mocking the idea, you're actually giving it more power. People who hesitate are often caught in their own traps of fear or laziness," Antonio explained.

"Please, continue. I can see in your eyes and expression that you have something significant to say, something that's difficult for you to express," Sebastian urged, now fully engaged.

. . .

Antonio laid out his thoughts clearly, "Consider this—our king, who is so forgettable and will be even more so when he's gone, has almost been convinced by Gonzalo's tales. Gonzalo, who only seems to excel at persuasion, has the king believing his son survived. But the reality that the prince might have survived is as unlikely as it is for the man sleeping here to be swimming."

Sebastian, somewhat resigned, admitted, "I have no hope that he's survived."

Antonio, seizing on his words, enthused, "But from that lack of hope, look at the immense opportunity before you! The absence of hope in one direction points us towards a path filled with such high hopes that ambition itself couldn't dream of what lies beyond. Let's agree, then, that Ferdinand is lost."

"He's gone," Sebastian confirmed, accepting the grim reality.

. . .

"Then who stands to inherit Naples next?" Antonio prodded, guiding Sebastian to the heart of their scheme.

"Claribel," Sebastian responded, recognizing the line of succession.

"Yes, Claribel, who's now the queen of Tunis, so far removed from us that communication seems impossible. She's as unreachable as if the sun had to deliver our messages, and even then, it would be too slow. She's distant, and from her departure, we all faced danger at sea. Yet, here we are, given a chance to act, with what has happened merely setting the stage for what we might do next," Antonio explained, painting a picture of opportunity from their circumstances.

Sebastian, puzzled by Antonio's words, asked for clarity, "What are you suggesting? It's true, my niece is queen of Tunis, and yes, she's the heir to Naples. But there's a vast distance between those places."

. . .

Antonio, ever persuasive, pressed on, "A distance so great it screams out for a solution. How could Claribel ever bridge that gap back to Naples? It's as if the very space itself suggests, 'Let Claribel stay in Tunis, and let Sebastian take action.' Imagine, if the current situation were permanent—if they were all out of the picture. They're no better to us now than if that were true. There are those among us who can govern Naples as well as the one who now sleeps; who can talk as much and as pointlessly as Gonzalo. I could match their empty words. Oh, if only you shared my perspective! This situation could be a turning point for you. Do you grasp what I'm suggesting?"

Sebastian, contemplating the gravity of Antonio's proposal, acknowledged, "I think I understand your point."

"And how does this revelation sit with your own aspirations?" Antonio prodded, aiming to gauge Sebastian's ambition.

. . .

Reflecting on Antonio's past actions, Sebastian noted, "You overthrew your brother Prospero."

"True," Antonio admitted without remorse. "And look at me now, dressed far better than I ever was. My brother's servants, who were once equals, now serve me."

Sebastian, considering the moral implications, questioned, "But what about your conscience?"

Antonio scoffed at the notion, "Conscience? If it were something as bothersome as a sore, it might trouble me. But I don't feel its pricks. Any guilt that could stand between me and my goals is as insignificant as sugar, easily dissolved before it can bother me. Here lies your own brother, no more significant than the ground he sleeps on. With a mere three inches of my sword, I could end his sleep forever. And you, by acting, could secure your position indefinitely, free from the critique of this cautious old man. The others will follow whatever we suggest, as easily as a cat drinks milk."

. . .

Moved by Antonio's resolve and his own burgeoning ambition, Sebastian declared, "Your example shall guide me. Just as you took Milan, I will claim Naples. Let's draw our swords together. One swift act will free you from your obligations, and I, as king, will honor you."

"Let's prepare," Antonio said, plotting the precise moment for their treachery. "When I raise my hand, you do the same, aiming for Gonzalo."

"Hold, a moment," Sebastian hesitated.

As they conspired quietly, Ariel, invisible and sent by Prospero, intervened to thwart their scheme. Whispering into Gonzalo's ear, the spirit sang a warning of the looming betrayal, urging him to wake and be vigilant, thus preserving the lives Prospero valued and maintaining the integrity of his plans.

. . .

Antonio, ready for action, whispered, "Let's act quickly."

At that moment, Gonzalo, stirred by Ariel's warning, prayed aloud, "Now, may good angels protect the king."

Alarmed by the sudden disturbance, everyone awoke. Alonso, confused and concerned, demanded, "What's happening? Why are your swords drawn? What caused such a fright?"

Gonzalo, equally puzzled, echoed, "What's going on?"

Sebastian, thinking quickly, fabricated a story, "While we were standing guard over your sleep, we were startled by a terrifying noise, like that of roaring lions. Didn't it wake you? It was truly horrifying."

. . .

"I didn't hear anything," Alonso admitted, still disoriented from sleep.

Antonio supported Sebastian's lie, "It was loud enough to scare a monster, to shake the very earth! It sounded like a pack of lions roaring."

Alonso turned to Gonzalo, seeking confirmation, "Did you hear this noise?"

Gonzalo, cautious yet honest, responded, "On my honor, sir, I did hear something strange that woke me. I tried to wake you, sir. When I opened my eyes, I saw their swords drawn. There definitely was a noise. It might be wise for us to be on guard, or perhaps we should leave this place. Let's ready our weapons, just in case."

Alonso, taking charge of the situation, decided, "Let's move from here and continue our search for my son."

. . .

"May the heavens protect him from whatever dangers lurk on this island, for he surely is here," Gonzalo hoped aloud.

With that, Alonso led the group away from the potential danger.

Ariel, satisfied with the intervention, thought to himself, "Prospero, my lord, will be pleased to know I've kept them safe. Now, the king can continue his search for his son without harm."

And with those words, they all exited, continuing their search across the island.

SCENE 2

Caliban stumbled through the island under the weight of his burden, muttering curses under his breath as thunder echoed in the distance. "Let every sickness the sun draws from the marshes fall upon Prospero," he spat. "He commands the spirits, yet I must curse him. They torment me with their tricks, pinching and leading me astray in the darkness, yet for every small mistake, their punishment awaits."

As he continued his tirade, Trinculo appeared, looking around bewilderedly at the brewing storm. "No shelter in sight, and this storm looks fierce,"

Trinculo said to himself, eyeing the ominous clouds. "What's this? A man or a fish? Dead or alive?" He prodded at Caliban. "Smells like a fish, a very ancient smell. In England, this would be a spectacle worth a silver piece."

Caliban, noticing Trinculo, thought him to be a spirit sent by Prospero to harass him for being slow. "I'll lay flat. Maybe he'll ignore me," Caliban reasoned, hoping to avoid further torment.

Trinculo, mistaking Caliban for a creature struck by lightning, decided to seek shelter under Caliban's cloak from the approaching storm. "Strange company is better than none in times of misery," he muttered, crawling next to Caliban.

Meanwhile, Stephano, singing drunkenly, stumbled upon them. "No more sea voyages for me; this island will be my end," he declared, taking another swig from his bottle. His song filled the air, a tune about sailors and their loves, a balm for his solitude.

. . .

Caliban groaned under his breath, "Please, don't torture me!"

Stephano, bemused, looked around. "What's this? Are we playing tricks now, summoning devils and exotic men? I didn't survive a shipwreck just to be scared of something on four legs. They say a brave man can stand on all fours and not back down. And I'll stand by that as long as I'm breathing."

"The spirit, it's torturing me," Caliban whimpered.

Stephano squinted at Caliban. "Here's a strange creature on the island, sick and shivering. How does he know our language? I'll help him out, if only for his ability to speak. Imagine the fortune if I could take him back to Naples. He'd be a gift fit for a king."

Caliban pleaded, "Just stop hurting me, and I'll bring my wood home faster."

. . .

Stephano, misunderstanding Caliban's fear for a sickness, said, "He's confused now, doesn't know what he's saying. Let's see if some wine might cure what ails him. If I can make him mine, tame him, there's money to be made."

"You're barely hurting me now, but soon you'll do more, I can tell by your shaking," Caliban said, believing Prospero was using Stephano to punish him.

"Come now, open up," Stephano insisted, offering his bottle. "This will cure your shakes, give you the gift of speech. You can't even tell friends from foes. Open up and drink."

Trinculo, recognizing Stephano's voice amidst his confusion, thought, "I know him, but it can't be—he drowned. These must be demons."

Stephano laughed, "A creature with four legs and two voices! Quite the curiosity! One voice praises, the other criticizes. If my wine can cure him, I'm all for it. Here's to your health!"

In this strange encounter, misunderstandings and hopes of fortune blend as Stephano and Trinculo navigate their unexpected meeting with Caliban, each interpreting the situation through their own lens of fear, curiosity, and greed.

Trinculo, desperate for familiarity, cried out, "Stephano!"

Stephano, bewildered, responded, "Is that another voice I hear? This must be a devil, not a creature. I should leave; I'm not equipped to deal with devils."

"It's me, Trinculo, your friend! Don't be afraid," Trinculo reassured, seeking to connect with Stephano.

. . .

Relieved, Stephano said, "Trinculo! Let me help you up. Only Trinculo could have such skinny legs. It's really you! But how did you end up under this creature?"

"I thought he was struck by lightning. But tell me, Stephano, did you survive the shipwreck? Are you not drowned?" Trinculo asked, filled with hope and surprise.

Stephano, a bit seasick from the ordeal, begged, "Please, let's not move too much. My stomach can't handle it."

Caliban, observing the scene, thought to himself, "These must be powerful beings, not spirits. This man has divine drink. I should pledge myself to him."

"How did you manage to survive?" Stephano asked, curious about Trinculo's tale.

. . .

"I clung to a barrel of wine that was thrown overboard. And you?" Stephano shared his own escape story.

"I swear allegiance to you and your magical bottle," Caliban declared, seeing an opportunity.

"And how did you escape, Trinculo?" Stephano turned to his friend.

"Swam like a duck to shore. I'm as good as any duck," Trinculo boasted.

Stephano, amused by the situation, offered his bottle as a makeshift 'book' for oaths. "Here, seal your loyalty with a kiss. Though you're as graceful in the water as a duck, you're as silly as a goose on land."

Trinculo, intrigued by the drink, eagerly asked, "Do you have more of this wonderful stuff?"

. . .

"All stored in a rock by the seaside, my makeshift cellar," Stephano boasted, turning to Caliban. "And how are you feeling, eh? Still shivering?"

Caliban, in awe, questioned, "Did you descend from the heavens?"

Stephano played along, "Straight from the moon, I assure you. I was the man in the moon once upon a time."

Caliban, filled with reverence, said, "I've seen you there! My mistress once showed me your image. I worship you!"

"Then swear loyalty to me," Stephano urged, improvising a ritual of allegiance.

Trinculo couldn't contain his amusement, mocking Caliban's naivety. "A shallow, gullible creature indeed! Scared of this? A weak, drunken fool! The man in the moon? Ha!"

Caliban, unfazed, promised Stephano, "I'll guide you through the island's riches and be your most loyal follower. Just let me worship you."

Trinculo, scoffing at the scene, remarked, "What a traitorous, tipsy monster! Waits for his god to sleep to steal his liquor."

"I swear to serve you faithfully," Caliban declared, ready to prostrate himself.

"Then let's make it official. Swear your allegiance," Stephano encouraged.

Trinculo found the entire spectacle hilarious, considering Caliban a simpleton. "I'm dying of laughter here. Such a foolish, pitiful creature."

. . .

"Come on, seal your oath with a kiss," Stephano prompted, caught up in his newfound power.

Trinculo, still mocking, added, "What a sorry state, driven to this by drink. A truly despicable monster."

Caliban, filled with newfound hope, promised Stephano an abundance of the island's riches. "I'll show you where the fresh water is, pick berries for you, catch fish, and gather wood. I'm done serving my cruel master. I'll follow you, miraculous man."

Trinculo couldn't help but mock the situation. "To think this monster marvels at a mere drunkard!"

But Caliban, undeterred, continued, "Let me take you to the crab-filled shores. With my own hands, I'll unearth nuts for you, show you where the birds nest, teach you to catch quick marmosets, fetch nuts, and even bring you baby seagulls from the cliffs. Will you come with me?"

. . .

Stephano, eager to explore these promises, urged, "Lead on, but let's keep moving without any more chatter. Trinculo, since we're the only ones left, we'll make this place ours. Hold my bottle; we'll have more to drink soon."

Caliban, overjoyed with his newfound freedom, sang boisterously, bidding farewell to his old life of servitude.

Trinculo laughed, "What a noisy, drunken spectacle he is!"

Caliban sang of his relief from his tedious tasks, embracing his new allegiance with joy, "No more labor for me under the old master. I've found a new one. Freedom is mine at last!"

Stephano, amused and intrigued by Caliban's offer and enthusiasm, declared, "Lead the way, noble creature."

. . .

Together, they set off, a strange fellowship bound by circumstance, each with their own dreams of what the island could offer them.

ACT III

SCENE 1

Ferdinand carried a heavy log, his muscles straining with the effort. He mused to himself, "Some tasks are tough, but finding joy in them makes all the difference. Even the most humble work can lead to great outcomes. This job, hauling these logs, could have been unbearable, but thinking of Miranda, the woman I work for, turns this chore into a joy. She's far kinder than her strict father, Prospero. Despite the daunting number of logs I must move as part of this task, Miranda's gentle presence makes the labor feel lighter. She even cries when she sees me work, claiming no one has ever performed such lowly tasks with such grace."

. . .

As he continued his work, Miranda approached, with Prospero watching from a distance, unnoticed.

Miranda, with a worried tone, pleaded, "Please, don't work so hard. I wish lightning would strike and burn these logs so you wouldn't have to carry them. Put it down and rest. My father won't notice; he's busy with his studies."

Ferdinand, looking up, replied warmly, "Dear Miranda, I won't be done before sunset."

"If you rest, I can carry the logs for a while," Miranda offered, reaching for the log.

Ferdinand gently refused, "No, I couldn't bear to see you lower yourself to such work while I sit idle."

Miranda insisted, "I want to help. It wouldn't demean me any more than it does you. I could do it easily, wanting to, whereas you're doing it out of obligation."

Prospero observed them from afar, his heart softened yet wary, "This sickness shows itself in such kindness."

Miranda, noticing the fatigue in Ferdinand's face, expressed her concern, "You look tired."

Ferdinand, heartened by her presence, assured her, "No, my noble lady, your company refreshes me, no matter the time of day. But please, could you tell me your name? I wish to include you in my prayers."

"Miranda," she confessed, with a glance towards where her father stood hidden. "I'm not supposed to reveal that, but now you know."

Ferdinand's admiration was evident. "Miranda, truly, you are a marvel, the very essence of beauty and virtue. I've met many women and admired their various qualities, but always found something lacking. But you— you're the culmination of all that's wonderful, without a single flaw."

Miranda, humble and innocent, replied, "I don't know much about the world, having seen no other women but myself in a mirror, and knowing no men but you and my father. I wouldn't want anyone else for company but you, unable to even imagine anyone else I could cherish."

Ferdinand, moved by her words, shared his own status. "I'm a prince, Miranda, and in my heart, I feel like a king. I'd endure anything, reject all forms of bondage, just to be near you. The moment I saw you, my heart pledged its service to you, making me willingly take on this labor for your sake."

Miranda, with a blend of hope and vulnerability, asked Ferdinand, "Do you love me?"

. . .

Ferdinand, with a passion that seemed to pull the very stars from the sky, proclaimed, "May heaven and earth witness my declaration! If my words are true, let them be blessed. If false, let them bring me ruin. I love you more than anything in this world, beyond any measure."

Miranda, overwhelmed by joy and tears, confessed, "I'm crying even though I'm happy."

Prospero, watching them, silently marveled at their deep affection, wishing them divine blessings.

"Why do you cry?" Ferdinand inquired, concerned.

Miranda, expressing her unworthiness, shared, "I feel too humble to offer what I wish to give, and even less worthy to receive what I deeply desire. But I won't play games. I'm straightforward in my innocence: I'll be your wife if you'll have me. If not, I'll remain devoted to you as your servant, regardless of your choice."

. . .

Ferdinand, moved by her sincerity, declared, "You are the dearest to me. I will always remain humble before you."

"Then, we're husband and wife?" Miranda sought confirmation.

"Yes, with all my heart," Ferdinand agreed, offering his hand as a sign of his commitment.

"And here's mine, with all my heart in it. Let's part for now and meet again in half an hour," Miranda proposed, sealing their pledge.

As they went their separate ways for the moment, Prospero, although not as outwardly jubilant as the young lovers, felt a deep sense of satisfaction. He knew there was much he still needed to do before the day ended and returned to his studies, his heart light with the events that had unfolded.

SCENE 2

Caliban, Stephano, and Trinculo found themselves wandering a different part of the island, their conversation as meandering as their path.

"Look, when we're out of booze, we'll just drink water. Not a single drop until then. So, keep it together and follow my lead," Stephano instructed, eyeing his strange companions. "Here, monster-servant, have a drink on me."

"Monster-servant? What a joke this island is!" Trinculo laughed. "They say only five of us are here.

With us three, if the other two are as smart as we are, this place is doomed."

"Listen, monster, drink when I tell you to. You look like you're about to pass out," Stephano chided.

Trinculo quipped, "Where else should his eyes be? Only a real freak of nature would have eyes on its tail."

Stephano, not missing a beat, boasted, "My monster here's drunk, but not me. I once swam for miles without drowning. Mark my words, you'll be my right-hand man, or maybe my flag-bearer."

"Right-hand man sounds about right; he's certainly no flag," Trinculo snorted.

"We're not running away, Mr. Monster," Stephano declared with a hiccup.

. . .

"Nor are we moving much at all. We might as well be dogs, lying around and saying nothing," Trinculo added, sprawled on the ground.

"Come on, say something for once, if you're a good monster," Stephano urged Caliban.

Caliban, looking up with a mix of reverence and desperation, replied, "How can I help you? I'd even kiss your shoes. But I won't follow him; he doesn't have courage."

"You're lying, you know nothing, monster!" Trinculo erupted. "I could outmaneuver a cop right now. You, a half-fish, half-monster, calling me a coward? After all the booze I've had today? Are you going to stand there and spout nonsense?"

Caliban turned to Stephano, feeling mocked by Trinculo's jibes, "See how he mocks me! Will you let him, my lord?"

. . .

Trinculo couldn't believe his ears, "My lord? To think a monster could be so naive!"

Again, Caliban pleaded, "He's doing it again! Please, bite him to death if you would."

Stephano warned Trinculo, "Keep your insults to yourself. If you start any trouble, you'll find yourself hanging from the next tree! Caliban here is under my protection, and I won't have you disrespecting him."

Caliban expressed his gratitude, "Thank you, my noble lord. Would you listen once more to the request I made?"

"Of course," Stephano agreed, ready to hear him out while Ariel, unseen by all, hovered nearby.

. . .

Caliban revisited his grievance, "As I've said, I'm under the control of a sorcerer who tricked me out of this island through his magic."

Ariel, invisible and indignant, whispered, "You're lying."

Caliban, unaware of Ariel's presence, retorted angrily to what he perceived as further mockery, "You lie, you mocking spirit! I wish my brave master would get rid of you! I'm not lying."

Stephano, misinterpreting the direction of Caliban's outburst, threatened Trinculo, "If you interrupt his story again, I swear I'll knock your teeth out."

Trinculo, confused, protested, "I didn't say anything!"

"Then keep quiet and let him finish," Stephano commanded.

. . .

Caliban continued, his voice heavy with the weight of his tale, "By his magic, he took this island from me. If you choose to avenge this wrong—I know you have the courage, unlike him—"

"That's for sure," Stephano interjected, confident in his ability to face any challenge.

"You shall rule this island, and I will serve you," Caliban promised, seeing in Stephano a chance to reclaim what he believed was rightfully his.

Stephano, intrigued by the plan, asked, "How can we make this happen? Can you lead me to him?"

"Yes, my lord. I can deliver him to you while he's asleep. Then, you can easily take care of him," Caliban promised eagerly.

Ariel, still unseen, taunted, "You're lying; you can't do that."

. . .

Caliban, mistaking the source of the taunt, lashed out, "What a fool! Please, hit him and take his bottle. Once it's gone, he'll be desperate for a drink and won't find any, because I won't show him where the fresh water is."

Stephano, misunderstanding the situation and thinking Trinculo was the one causing trouble again, warned, "Trinculo, don't push your luck. Interrupt again, and I'll forget my kindness and treat you harshly."

"I didn't do anything. I'll just stay back," Trinculo replied, distancing himself from the conflict.

"Didn't you accuse him of lying?" Stephano questioned, still confused about who spoke.

Ariel whispered again, "You're lying."

. . .

Stephano, thinking it was Trinculo's voice, reacted impulsively and struck Trinculo. "Take that! And if you dare to call me a liar again, you'll get worse."

"I didn't say anything! Have you lost your mind? Cursed be your drinking and your monster too!" Trinculo retorted, feeling wronged and frustrated.

Caliban laughed at the chaos.

"Continue with your story. But keep your distance," Stephano ordered, eager to hear more about the plan.

Caliban, somewhat satisfied, added, "You've beaten him enough. Maybe later, I'll have a go at him too."

Stephano, eager to hear more, urged, "Move back a bit. Now, keep talking."

. . .

Caliban explained his plan further, "Like I said, he usually sleeps in the afternoon. That's your chance to get him. You could hit him with a log, stab him, or just cut his throat. But first, grab his books. Without his magic books, he's nothing—a fool, just like me. He can't control anything without them. Everyone hates him as much as I do. Just burn his books. He calls his magic tools 'brave utensils.' He plans to decorate his home with them. And his daughter, he thinks she's unmatched. I've only ever seen my mother Sycorax and her, but she's far more beautiful."

"Is she that beautiful?" Stephano was intrigued.

"Yes, my lord. She'd be a perfect match for you, and your children would be magnificent," Caliban assured him.

"Monster, I'll go through with it. His daughter and I will rule as king and queen, with you and Trinculo as our deputies. What do you think of that, Trinculo?" Stephano was getting carried away by the plot.

. . .

"Sounds great," Trinculo agreed, still a bit wary.

"Give me your hand. I'm sorry for hitting you earlier. Just remember to watch your tongue," Stephano said, offering a gesture of reconciliation.

"He'll be asleep within half an hour. Will you do it then?" Caliban was eager to see the plan set into motion.

"I swear on my honor," Stephano committed.

Ariel, listening to every word, thought, "I'll report this to my master."

Caliban, visibly pleased with the turn of events, suggested, "Let's celebrate. Sing that song you taught me earlier."

. . .

At Caliban's request, Stephano agreed to a moment of levity, "For you, monster, I'll indulge. Trinculo, let's sing."

The trio attempted a song, their voices rough but eager:
"Mock them and jeer them,
Jeer them and mock them,
Thoughts are free."

"That's not right," Caliban noted, hearing the melody amiss.

Suddenly, Ariel, unseen, played the correct tune, enchanting the air.

"What's this?" Stephano wondered, confused by the unseen music.

Trinculo, equally baffled, joked, "It's the tune of our song, played by an invisible musician."

. . .

"If you're a man, show yourself. If you're a devil, do as you please," Stephano challenged the air.

Trinculo, scared, prayed for forgiveness.

Stephano, trying to be brave, declared, "Death clears all debts. I'm not afraid of you. Have mercy on us!"

Caliban, noticing their fear, asked, "Are you scared?"

"Not me," Stephano denied.

"There's no need to be afraid," Caliban reassured them. "The island is alive with sounds and music that don't mean any harm. Sometimes, it feels like the air is full of music and voices that lull me to sleep, and in my dreams, I see riches that make me wish to sleep forever."

. . .

Stephano, intrigued by the magic of the island, mused, "This place will be a fine kingdom for me, filled with endless music."

"But only after we deal with Prospero," Caliban reminded him.

"That'll happen in time. I remember our plan," Stephano said, determined.

As the music faded, Trinculo suggested, "Let's follow the sound, and then we can carry out our task."

"Lead the way, monster. I'm curious to see this musician," Stephano said, intrigued by the island's mysteries.

"Are we going? I'll follow you, Stephano," Trinculo decided, ready to see where this adventure would take them.

. . .

And with that, they exited, following the haunting melody that wove through the island's air, their plot against Prospero simmering in the background.

SCENE 3

Gonzalo, panting and out of breath, announced he couldn't walk another step. "My old bones are aching. This place is like a labyrinth!" he complained, looking for a spot to rest.

Alonso, feeling the weight of his own tiredness, agreed. "I'm just as worn out," he admitted. "Let's all take a moment to rest. I've given up hope anyway. The one we're searching for is probably lost to the sea by now."

. . .

Antonio whispered to Sebastian, barely hiding his delight. "See, he's lost all hope. Don't let this setback stop us from what we've planned."

"To the next opportunity then," Sebastian whispered back, conspiratorially.

"Let's make our move tonight," Antonio suggested. "They're all exhausted, less alert."

"Tonight, then. No delays," Sebastian agreed, settling on their secret plan.

Suddenly, the air filled with enchanting music, drawing everyone's attention. "Listen to that beautiful sound!" Alonso exclaimed, intrigued.

"It's wonderful!" Gonzalo agreed, equally captivated.

. . .

As they marveled, an invisible Prospero watched from afar while mysterious figures appeared, setting a magical feast before them and then vanishing as quickly as they came.

"What was that?" Alonso wondered aloud, astonished by the sight.

Sebastian couldn't hide his amazement. "It's like a fantasy come to life. I'm starting to believe in unicorns and that somewhere, a phoenix rules from its tree," he said, his imagination captured by the magic of the moment.

Antonio, caught up in the moment, declared, "I'm willing to believe that and anything else just as fantastic. Travelers have seen wonders that those who stay at home wouldn't believe."

Gonzalo mused aloud, "If I were to tell this story back in Naples, who would believe me? That I saw inhabitants of this island, of strange appearance, yet their behavior was more gentle and kind than many people I know."

Prospero, hidden and listening, thought to himself, "You speak the truth, Gonzalo. Some here are indeed worse than devils."

Alonso couldn't stop marveling at the sight. "Such beings, their movements, and the sounds they made, communicated so much, even without speech. It was like a profound silent conversation."

"Compliments are easy as one leaves," Prospero noted to himself, impressed yet cynical.

Francisco remarked on how mysteriously the figures had disappeared.

Sebastian, ever practical, said, "No matter how they left, they left us food. Why not eat what's here?"

. . .

Alonso declined, feeling uneasy.

But Gonzalo encouraged, "There's no need to be wary. Remember the tales we believed as boys? About men with heads in their chests or mountain dwellers with bull-like features? Now, we accept them as truth based on evidence brought back by travelers."

Feeling resigned, Alonso agreed to eat. "Might as well enjoy what we can. The best may already be behind us. Come, let's eat together."

As they were about to eat, the atmosphere shifted dramatically with thunder and lightning heralding the arrival of Ariel, appearing as a harpy. With a dramatic flap of his wings, the banquet vanished into thin air.

"You are three sinners, singled out by fate," Ariel thundered, addressing them directly. "The endless sea has spat you out onto this uninhabited island, where you, the least deserving of life among men, have been driven to madness. Your attempts to harm me or my kind with your swords might as well be attempts to slash the wind or stab the water—they're pointless."

Alonso, Sebastian, and the others, driven by a mix of fear and defiance, drew their swords, but their gestures were futile.

Ariel continued, unphased, "Remember, you three conspired against Prospero, rightful Duke of Milan, casting him and his innocent daughter to the mercy of the sea. This act of treachery has not been forgotten by the elements themselves, which now conspire against you. Alonso, your son is taken from you as retribution. What awaits you is a fate worse than death, step by excruciating step, unless you find redemption through deep remorse and a change of heart."

With that ominous warning, Ariel vanished as suddenly as he appeared, leaving behind a stunned silence broken only by the return of the mysterious figures, their dance mocking the solemnity of the moment.

Prospero, observing from afar, praised Ariel's performance, "Well done, Ariel. You've conveyed my message perfectly, not missing a beat of what I taught you. My plan is coming together; they are now completely under my influence, lost in their guilt and fear. It's time to visit Ferdinand, who they believe is dead, my beloved child and his."

As Prospero exited, Gonzalo, deeply shaken, turned to the others, asking in a voice filled with confusion and fear, "In the name of all that is sacred, what has just happened to us?"

Alonso was overwhelmed, his voice trembling with emotion. "It's beyond belief," he exclaimed. "The very waves seemed to speak to me, the winds sang out the tale, and the thunder, like a powerful organ, announced Prospero's name, underscoring my guilt. My son must be lying beneath the waves, and I will search deeper than anyone has ever searched, even if it means joining him in his watery grave." With a heavy heart, he left to begin his impossible search.

Sebastian, trying to muster some bravado, declared, "I'll take them on one by one, even if their numbers are legion."

Antonio quickly offered his support, "I'll stand by you." Together, they followed Alonso out.

Gonzalo observed the scene with a heavy heart. "They're acting out of desperation, driven by the enormity of their guilt which, like a slow-working poison, is now starting to take its toll. I urge those of you who can move quickly to follow them and prevent them from doing something they might regret in this state of frenzy."

Adrian agreed, understanding the urgency, "Let's follow them and see what can be done." They hurried out, hoping to avert further tragedy.

ACT IV

SCENE 1

Prospero, Ferdinand, and Miranda were standing outside Prospero's home when Prospero began to speak. "I might have punished you harshly, Ferdinand, but now I make it up to you. I'm giving you something very precious to me, as valuable as my own life—the love of my daughter, Miranda. All the challenges I put you through were just to test your love for her, and you've proven yourself worthy. Here, in front of Heaven itself, I confirm this precious gift to you. And Ferdinand, don't think I'm just bragging about my daughter. You'll find she's beyond all the praise you might hear, lagging far behind her true worth."

. . .

Ferdinand, moved by Prospero's words, replied, "I'd trust your words over any prophecy."

Prospero continued, "So, as my gift to you, and through your own efforts, you've rightly earned my daughter. But, if you dishonor her before the wedding is properly celebrated, expect no blessings from above. Instead, your marriage will be cursed with hate, disdain, and discord. So, be careful and let the wedding be your guide."

Ferdinand responded earnestly, "I promise, with the hope of a peaceful and prosperous life ahead, that no temptation could ever make me dishonor her. The celebration of our wedding day will be sacred, and nothing could tarnish it."

"Nicely said," Prospero nodded in approval. "Now, go sit and talk with her; she's yours." Then, calling out, "Ariel, my hardworking servant, Ariel!"

. . .

The Tempest

Ariel appeared in an instant. "What do you need, master? I'm here."

Prospero turned his attention to Ariel and said, "You and your lesser companions did a great job last time, and I need your skills again. Go gather your group and bring them here. I have given you the authority over them. Make them move quickly; I've promised to show this young couple a bit of my magic, and they're expecting it."

"Do you want it done right now?" Ariel asked.

"Yes, immediately," Prospero replied.

Ariel, full of spirit, promised a swift return, "Before you can even complete a thought, and before you can breathe out twice or say 'just so,' I'll have everyone here, ready and making faces. Do you doubt my loyalty, master?"

. . .

Prospero expressed his affection, "My dear Ariel, I treasure you. Just wait for my call before you show up."

"I understand," Ariel said before vanishing.

Prospero then cautioned Ferdinand, "Stay true to your word. Don't let passion take over. Even the strongest promises can burn up in the heat of desire. Be careful, or your vows mean nothing."

Ferdinand reassured him, "I promise, sir. The purity in my heart cools any hot impulse."

Satisfied, Prospero called for Ariel again, "Now, my Ariel, bring more than just a few spirits if you have to. Show up and make a spectacle, but no sound. All eyes should be on you, in silence."

As the soft music played, Iris appeared with a flourish. "Ceres, bountiful lady, your lands are rich with crops, your mountains home to sheep, and your meadows lush. Your riverbanks are beautifully adorned, awaiting April's touch to bloom. You've made nature a haven for the heartbroken and a paradise for growth. Now, Juno, the queen of the sky and my mistress, calls you to leave these wonders for a moment. She invites you to this grassy field to entertain and celebrate."

Ceres then made her entrance, her presence as majestic as the nature she governed. "Welcome, Iris, colorful messenger of Jupiter, who never strays from his wife's side. Your arrival brings sweetness to my fields and crowns my lands with your rainbow's end. But tell me, why has your queen called me here to this well-groomed lawn?"

Iris was quick to respond, "We're here to honor a commitment of true love, to bless the union of two hearts with the gifts of nature and joy."

Ceres, her curiosity piqued, pressed further, "But is Venus or her son lurking around? Their mischief with my daughter has made me wary of their presence."

Iris assured her, "Fear not, for Venus and her son are far from here, headed towards Paphos. Their schemes hold no power today. The couple we celebrate has vowed to honor their love purely, leaving no room for Venus's temptations."

Ceres, relieved by Iris's words, prepared to bless the event, content in the knowledge that the celebration would remain untainted by the gods of love's usual antics.

As they stood together, Ceres noticed someone approaching. "Look, the highest queen, Great Juno, is coming. I can tell by the way she walks."

Juno arrived with a grandeur that filled the space. "How are you, generous sister? Come with me to bless this couple so they may have a prosperous and respected future."

. . .

Together, they began to sing, their voices intertwining with the magic of the moment.

Juno started, "I wish you honor, wealth, and a marriage full of blessings. May your life together grow stronger over time, and may happiness follow you every hour. These are the blessings I, Juno, give you."

Ceres joined in, "May the earth yield its bounty to you, your storerooms always full. May your vines bear fruit, and your fields produce abundantly. May the springtime of your love last until the harvest's end, and may you never know need. This is my blessing upon you."

Ferdinand, overwhelmed by the spectacle, remarked, "This vision is majestic, and the harmony is enchantingly beautiful. Could these be spirits?"

. . .

Prospero, pleased with the effect, replied, "Yes, spirits summoned by my magic to fulfill our imaginations for this celebration."

Ferdinand, moved by the experience, exclaimed, "I wish to stay here forever. Such a father and a wife turn this place into a paradise."

Meanwhile, Juno and Ceres conferred quietly, sending Iris on a task with whispers that hinted at more to come.

Prospero called for silence, "Quiet now! Juno and Ceres are plotting something. We mustn't interrupt, or the spell will be broken."

Iris called out to the nymphs of the winding streams, with their crowns of sedge and gentle gaze, to leave their flowing waters and come to the green land at Juno's command. "Come, mild nymphs, and join us in celebrating a true love's agreement. Don't be late."

. . .

As the nymphs arrived, Iris then beckoned the tanned reapers, tired from their August labors, to come and be merry. "Put on your straw hats and join these fresh nymphs in a dance of the countryside."

The reapers, dressed for the occasion, merged with the nymphs in a graceful dance. Just as the celebration reached its peak, Prospero was jolted by a sudden remembrance of Caliban's plot against him. He whispered to himself about the imminent danger of their scheme.

To the spirits, he abruptly commanded, "Well done! Enough; vanish now."

Ferdinand, noticing Prospero's sudden change, remarked, "This is odd. Your father seems deeply affected by some strong emotion."

Miranda, concerned, added, "I've never seen him so disturbed and angry before."

. . .

Prospero, trying to reassure them, said, "You seem worried, Ferdinand. Cheer up. Our celebration is now over. All the performers you saw were merely spirits, and they have dissolved into thin air, just like this grand illusion will fade away, leaving nothing behind. Everything in our world, including the world itself, is as fleeting as a dream, and our lives are just a brief moment within a larger sleep. I'm a bit upset, forgive me; my mind is troubled. Don't let my mood disturb you. If you'd like, you can rest in my home while I take a walk to calm my thoughts."

Ferdinand and Miranda, sensing Prospero's need for solitude, expressed their wishes for his peace before leaving him to his thoughts.

Prospero, now alone, called out for Ariel with a mere thought. "Ariel, come to me with your quickness."

Ariel appeared instantly, in tune with Prospero's wishes. "I'm always aligned with your thoughts. What do you need?"

. . .

"We have to deal with Caliban and his plot," Prospero informed him.

"Yes, my leader. When I was disguising as Ceres, I almost brought it up, but I was worried it might upset you," Ariel admitted.

"Where did you last see them?" Prospero inquired about Caliban and his co-conspirators.

Ariel recounted, "I left them drunk with courage, striking at the air for daring to touch their faces, cursing the ground for not worshiping their steps. They were still focused on their plan when I lured them with my drum. Like wild horses at the sound, they perked up, sniffing the air for music. I led them through thorns and brambles, cutting their legs, until they were dancing knee-deep in a stinking pond near your home, trapped by the illusion."

. . .

"Well done," Prospero praised. "Stay invisible and bring the flashy stuff from my house as bait to trap these thieves."

"I'm on it," Ariel replied, vanishing to carry out the task.

Prospero, with a tone of finality, lamented, "A devil, truly born a devil, who cannot be taught or changed, no matter how hard I try. All my efforts, meant kindly, are completely wasted on him. As he grows older, his body becomes more repulsive, and his mind more corrupt. I'll make them suffer, all of them, until they're screaming."

As Prospero plotted his revenge, Ariel returned, burdened with shiny clothes and other trinkets, and began to hang them on a line as instructed, both remaining unseen.

Then, Caliban, Stephano, and Trinculo, all soaked through, tiptoed onto the scene. "Quietly," Caliban urged, "we're near his home now. We mustn't make a sound."

Stephano, annoyed, complained, "Monster, this 'harmless' fairy of yours has made fools of us."

Trinculo chimed in with disgust, "I can smell nothing but horse urine; it's revolting."

"And I'm just as offended," Stephano added. "Listen here, monster, if I were to get angry with you..."

"You'd be nothing but a lost cause," Trinculo cut in.

Caliban, trying to keep the peace, pleaded, "My lord, stay on my side. Be patient, and the treasure I lead you to will make up for this mishap. So, let's speak quietly. It's as silent as midnight."

. . .

Trinculo, still fuming about their earlier mishap, said, "But to lose our bottles in that pond..."

"There's not just shame in that, monster, but a huge loss," Stephano lamented.

"That's worse to me than being soaked," Trinculo added, scornfully.

"I'll get our bottle back, even if it means drowning in the effort," Stephano declared, determined.

Caliban, with urgency in his voice, whispered to Stephano, "Please, my king, be quiet. Look, we're right at the entrance to the cell. Let's go in quietly and do the deed that will make this island yours forever. And I'll be forever loyal to you."

Stephano, intrigued by the promise of power, responded, "Give me your hand. I'm starting to feel quite violent."

The Tempest

. . .

Just then, Trinculo spotted the glistening apparel hanging on the line and exclaimed, "Oh king Stephano! Look at these clothes waiting for you!"

Caliban snapped at him, "Ignore it, you idiot. It's just rubbish."

But Trinculo, dazzled by the sight, insisted, "We know what these are good for. Right, King Stephano?"

Easily distracted, Stephano decided, "Take off that gown, Trinculo. I want it."

"Of course, your majesty," Trinculo agreed, eager to please.

Caliban, frustrated, muttered, "May you drown in your foolishness! Why focus on this junk? Let's do what we came for. If Prospero wakes up, he'll torture us horribly."

"Quiet, monster," Stephano silenced him, now preoccupied with a jerkin. "Isn't this my jacket? Ah, it's about to lose its lining."

Trinculo encouraged the theft, "Yes, let's take it all. It suits you, your grace."

Stephano, amused by the joke, rewarded Trinculo, "For that jest, you get a garment. I'll always reward wit while I'm the king here. 'Steal by line and level'—what a clever trick! Here's another piece for you."

Trinculo, trying to keep the momentum, said to Caliban, "Come on, let's get moving. Put some of this stuff on and let's take the rest."

. . .

But Caliban resisted, "I don't want any part of it. We're just wasting time. We'll either turn into barnacles or apes with shamefully low foreheads."

Stephano, seeing an opportunity, ordered, "Monster, get to work. Help carry this to where my wine is stored, or I'll banish you from my realm. Move it, take this."

"And this," Trinculo added, piling more items.

"Yes, take everything," Stephano commanded.

Suddenly, the air filled with the sounds of a hunt. Spirits, shaped like dogs and hounds, appeared, driven by Prospero and Ariel, chasing Caliban, Stephano, and Trinculo.

Prospero cheered them on, "Go, chase them down!"

. . .

Ariel joined in, "There they go! After them!"

Prospero called out, "Catch them, Fury! Get the tyrant!"

As Caliban, Stephano, and Trinculo were hounded out, Prospero gave another command to Ariel, "Tell my spirits to torment them with cramps and spasms, to mark them more than any wild animal."

Ariel noted, "Listen to their cries!"

Prospero, satisfied with the chase, declared, "Let them be pursued thoroughly. Now, all my foes are at my mercy. Soon, my work here will be done, and Ariel, you'll be free to roam the air. Just follow me a bit longer and serve me till the end." And with that, they exited, leaving the chaos of the hunt behind.

ACT V

SCENE 1

Prospero, wearing his magic robes, stood outside his cell with Ariel, his loyal spirit.

"Now, everything is coming together," Prospero said with a sense of accomplishment. "My magic is strong, the spirits listen to me, and everything is on schedule. What time is it?"

"It's six o'clock, my lord," Ariel replied. "You said that's when our task should end."

. . .

"Yes, I remember saying that when I first conjured the storm. Tell me, how are the king and his group doing?"

"They're exactly where you left them, trapped in the grove near your cell, just as you ordered. They can't move until you free them. The king, his brother, and yours are all beside themselves with worry, and the others are filled with sorrow. Especially the one you call 'the good old lord Gonzalo'; he's crying so much."

"Do you think I'd feel sorry for them if I saw them now?" Prospero asked.

"If I were human, I certainly would," Ariel admitted.

"So will I," Prospero decided. "If you, a spirit, feel a hint of their suffering, shouldn't I, being human, feel it even more? Despite their wrongs against me, I choose to act with compassion over revenge. They've shown remorse, and that's all I wanted. Go, free them, Ariel. I'll break my spells and give them back their senses. They'll be themselves again."

Ariel left to gather the captives, and Prospero turned his attention to the forces of nature, addressing the spirits and elements that had served his will.

"I'm giving up my magic," he declared to the unseen forces around him. "With your help, I've controlled the sun at noon, summoned storms, and even woke the dead. But now, I renounce all my spells and powers. After one last task, I'll break my magic staff and bury it deep in the earth, and my book of spells will be drowned deeper than any anchor can reach."

As solemn music filled the air, Ariel returned, leading Alonso and his companions, who were all under Prospero's spell, into a magical circle. They were dazed, caught in a limbo between realities.

. . .

"May this music heal your troubled minds," Prospero said, looking at them. "You've been caught in a spell, but now, the fog lifts from your brains."

He turned to Gonzalo, his eyes filled with tears of gratitude. "Dear Gonzalo, you saved my life and have always been loyal. I'll repay your kindness in both words and actions."

Then he addressed Alonso. "You treated me and my daughter cruelly, Alonso. Your brother helped you. And Sebastian, you let ambition blind you. But I forgive you all, even though it goes against nature. Your senses are returning, clearing like a tide washing away mud."

Prospero signaled Ariel. "Bring me my normal clothes. It's time to let go of this magic and present myself as the Duke of Milan once again. Soon, Ariel, you'll be free."

. . .

As the captives slowly came to their senses, Prospero prepared to reveal himself, ready to let go of the island's magic and return to his rightful place in the world.

As Ariel dressed him, the spirit sang a light-hearted song about the joy of living freely in nature, moving from one delight to another with the seasons. Prospero, now looking more like the Duke of Milan than a sorcerer, smiled fondly at Ariel. "My dear Ariel, I'll miss you, but you've earned your freedom," he said warmly. "Now, go to the king's ship. You'll find the crew asleep, but make sure the captain and boatswain are awake and bring them here immediately."

Ariel promised to return swiftly and disappeared to complete the task.

Gonzalo, overwhelmed by the unfolding events, prayed for divine guidance to lead them from this bewildering place. Prospero then turned to Alonso, revealing his true identity. "I am Prospero, the Duke of Milan you wronged. To prove I'm not a ghost or illusion, I welcome you with an embrace," he said, stepping forward to greet Alonso and his companions.

Alonso, stunned, struggled to reconcile this reality. "Are you really Prospero? I can hardly believe it. My mind has been so troubled; I thought I was going mad. If this is real, it's a most incredible story. I give up your dukedom and ask for your forgiveness for all I've done wrong. But how are you alive and here?"

Prospero, embracing Gonzalo, spoke with warmth and respect. "My dear friend, your honor is boundless. Let's not dwell on the past but look to the future and the peace we can bring to our lands and our hearts."

Gonzalo looked around, bewildered, and whispered, "I'm not sure if I can believe my own eyes."

. . .

Prospero, with a gentle smile, replied, "The island still plays tricks on your senses. But rest assured, you are most welcome here, my friends."

He then leaned closer to Sebastian and Antonio, his voice taking on a sharper edge. "As for you two, I could easily reveal your plots and label you traitors. But let's not dwell on that now."

Sebastian scoffed under his breath, "He's speaking nonsense."

Prospero, overhearing, calmly stated, "No, Sebastian. To my brother, who's wronged me deeply, I offer my forgiveness, though it pains me to even address you as such. And remember, you owe me my dukedom."

Alonso, caught in the moment, earnestly asked, "Prospero, can you tell us how you survived? It's been a shock, finding you here after we lost everything in the shipwreck, including my dear son Ferdinand."

. . .

"I'm truly sorry for your loss," Prospero replied, his voice soft with empathy.

Alonso, his grief surfacing, said, "It's a wound beyond healing."

"But maybe you haven't sought the right kind of help," Prospero suggested gently. "I too have suffered a great loss, as dear to me as yours, for I have lost my daughter."

Alonso, grasping at the notion of Prospero's lost daughter, lamented, "If only both our children were alive and well in Naples, away from this tragedy."

Prospero, with a calm demeanor, responded, "I lost her during the recent storm. It seems my revelations have left you all in awe, doubting your own senses. But I assure you, I am Prospero, the rightful Duke of Milan, cast away and landed here by fate."

. . .

He gestured around him, "This cell is now my court, and my kingdom is not what it once was. But since my dukedom is restored to me, I have a surprise that will hopefully please you as much as it does me."

As he spoke, Prospero revealed Ferdinand and Miranda, deeply engaged in a game of chess.

Miranda playfully accused Ferdinand, "You're cheating!"

Ferdinand, looking at her fondly, insisted, "I wouldn't cheat you for anything."

Miranda countered, "Even if it meant winning twenty kingdoms, it would still be a fair game to me."

Alonso, witnessing this, feared he was dreaming, "If this is just an illusion, then I'm losing my son all over again."

. . .

Sebastian, amazed, declared, "This is truly a miracle!"

Ferdinand, overwhelmed by the turn of events, gratefully acknowledged the mercy of the seas despite his earlier curses. He knelt, a gesture of respect and relief.

Alonso, embracing the joy of reunion, blessed his son. "Stand up and tell us how you arrived here."

Miranda, in awe of the new faces around her, exclaimed, "What a wonder! How many lovely people are here! How beautiful mankind is! Oh, what a wonderful new world that has such people in it!"

Prospero softly reminded her, "It's new to you."

Alonso, curious about the young woman engaging his son, asked, "Who is this lady you were playing with? You've only known each other for a short while. Is she the divine force that separated us and brought us together again?"

Ferdinand proudly introduced Miranda as mortal, yet divinely appointed as his. "She is the daughter of the Duke of Milan, from whom I've received a new life and a second father. Her father has given me a chance at a life I never thought possible."

Alonso, moved by the revelation, realized the strangeness of asking his own child for forgiveness.

Prospero, ever the peacemaker, suggested they leave the past behind. "Let's not weigh ourselves down with what's already passed."

Gonzalo, tearfully joyful, prayed for divine blessings on Ferdinand and Miranda. "May the gods bless this union, for it was their will that led us here."

. . .

Alonso responded with a hearty, "Amen, Gonzalo!"

Gonzalo, filled with wonder, exclaimed, "Who would have thought that Milan's exile would lead his offspring to become rulers of Naples? We should celebrate this unique joy, etch it in gold and remember forever. Claribel found a husband in Tunis, and here, Ferdinand finds a wife where he was lost. Prospero regains his dukedom on this sparse island, and all of us find ourselves when we thought all was lost."

Alonso, moved by the moment, reached out to Ferdinand and Miranda. "Anyone who doesn't wish you both every happiness must be heartless."

Gonzalo joyfully agreed, "Let it be so! Amen!"

Just then, Ariel reappeared, leading the ship's master and boatswain, both looking utterly confused and amazed.

. . .

"Look, sir, more of our crew!" Gonzalo pointed out. "I joked that this man couldn't drown unless we had a gallows on land. What's the silence for now? Can't you speak on land? What happened?"

The boatswain, still in disbelief, shared their miraculous tale. "The best news is we've found our king and his party. And our ship, which we thought was lost, is now in perfect condition, as good as when we first set sail."

Ariel whispered to Prospero, proudly admitting to orchestrating these events.

Prospero, quietly praising Ariel, replied, "You've outdone yourself, my clever spirit!"

Alonso, overwhelmed by these unnatural occurrences, sought clarity. "How did you end up here?"

. . .

The boatswain tried to explain, "Honestly, sir, if I weren't wide awake, I'd think I was dreaming. We were all put to sleep, and next thing we knew, we were here, with our ship as splendid as ever, as if by some enchantment, we were brought right here."

Ariel, seeking approval, whispered to Prospero, "Did I do well?"

Prospero, impressed, whispered back, "Exceptionally well, my hard worker. You'll soon be free."

Alonso, marveling at the situation, said, "This is the most bewildering experience I've ever had. There's something supernatural guiding this, something beyond mere nature."

Prospero reassured him, "My king, don't trouble your mind over the oddity of these events. I promise, soon, I'll explain everything in a way that will make sense to you. Until then, stay positive and see the good in what has happened."

. . .

Then, turning to Ariel, Prospero ordered, "Now, go and free Caliban and his two companions from their enchantment."

As Ariel left to carry out the task, Prospero turned to his guests, "How are you feeling, my lord? There are a few of your men still missing, but they'll be here shortly."

Ariel returned, herding Caliban, Stephano, and Trinculo in their ridiculous outfits, much to the amusement of everyone.

Stephano, trying to stay upbeat, declared, "Every man for himself, but let's not worry; it's all fortune's doing. Cheer up, my monster, cheer up!"

Trinculo, looking at his companions, joked, "If my eyes don't deceive me, this is quite the spectacle."

. . .

Caliban, somewhat ashamed and impressed by the grandeur of his master, Prospero, feared retribution, "Oh, these spirits are magnificent! Look how noble my master looks. I'm worried he might punish me."

Sebastian laughed, asking Antonio, "What are these creatures, my lord? Can we buy them with money?"

Antonio, eyeing Caliban, couldn't resist a jibe, "He looks like a fish you'd find in the market, doesn't he?"

Prospero, addressing the bewildered group, said, "Take a good look at these men. This deformed rogue here, his mother was a witch, powerful enough to control the moon's tides. They tried to rob me, and this half-demon even plotted to take my life. These other two, you know them, don't you? This creature of darkness, he's mine to claim."

Caliban muttered worriedly, "I'm in for it now."

. . .

Alonso, recognizing his servant, asked incredulously, "Isn't this Stephano, my butler? And how did he get so drunk?"

Sebastian chimed in with a laugh, "And where did they get such strong drink?"

Alonso turned to Trinculo, "And you, reeking of alcohol too? What's happened to you since we last saw you?"

Trinculo, looking miserable, replied, "I've been in such a state, I doubt I'll ever be clean again. I'm more worried about rotting than being blown away by the wind."

Sebastian couldn't help but tease Stephano, "Look at you, Stephano!"

Stephano, still playing his part, groaned, "Oh, don't touch me; I've turned into a cramp."

. . .

Prospero then mockingly asked, "So, you wanted to be king of the island, eh?"

Stephano, realizing his folly, admitted, "That would have turned out painfully."

Alonso, observing Caliban, remarked, "I've never seen anything like this before."

Prospero nodded, "His behavior is as ugly as his appearance. Take your friends and clean my cell. Do it well if you expect my forgiveness."

Caliban, with a new resolve, declared, "Yes, I'll do it. I'll be smarter from now on and look for kindness instead. How foolish I was to think that drunkard was a deity and to worship such an idiot!"

Prospero dismissed him with a wave, "Off you go!"

. . .

Alonso added, "Take your stolen goods back where you found them."

Sebastian couldn't resist a parting shot, "Or where you stole them from, more likely."

With that, Caliban, Stephano, and Trinculo left to make amends.

Prospero then turned to his guests, "Your Highness, I invite you and your company to spend the night in my modest dwelling. I'll share the tale of my life and the events that brought me here. In the morning, I'll guide you to your ship and then on to Naples. I hope to witness the wedding of our beloved children there. Afterward, I'll return to Milan, where I'll spend my days in peaceful reflection."

Alonso expressed eagerness to hear Prospero's story, expecting it to be extraordinary.

. . .

Prospero assured him, "I'll tell you everything. And I promise you a smooth journey back, with favorable winds to speed you on your way."

Turning to Ariel, Prospero gave his final command, "My Ariel, ensure their journey is safe. After that, you're free. Farewell."

He then invited everyone to follow him, as they exited towards Prospero's cell, ready to rest and prepare for the journey back to Naples and the celebrations that awaited them.

EPILOGUE

Prospero stood before his audience, the power of his magic no longer swirling around him.

"All my magical abilities have come to an end," he began, his voice reflecting a hint of weariness. "What little strength I have is purely my own, and honestly, it's not much. It's true, I'm at a crossroads. You can either keep me trapped here, or allow me to return to Naples. I've reclaimed my position as duke and forgiven those who wronged me. I shouldn't have to remain on this empty island because of magic. I'm asking for your help to free me."

. . .

He looked around at the faces before him.

"Your applause, your approval, is like a gentle wind that can set my sails moving again. Without it, everything I've worked for falls apart. My goal was always to entertain you. But now, I find myself running out of the energy and skill needed to enchant. I'm facing utter despair unless your prayers, which can reach even the heavens, come to my aid. Just as you hope to be forgiven for your mistakes, please, let your kindness release me from this predicament."

THE END

FURTHER READING

Shakespeare's Final Solo Play: "The Tempest" is believed to be the last play Shakespeare wrote alone, around 1610-1611. Its themes of reconciliation, forgiveness, and the nature of power are often interpreted as Shakespeare reflecting on his own life and career.

Island as a Microcosm: The setting of "The Tempest" on a remote island serves as a microcosm for society and human behavior. This isolation allows Shakespeare to explore themes of authority, freedom, and transformation in a controlled environment.

. . .

Prospero's Books and Magic: Prospero's use of magical books and spells is central to the plot, symbolizing knowledge and power. His decision to renounce magic at the play's end is seen as a metaphor for Shakespeare's own farewell to playwriting.

Colonialism and Postcolonial Readings: Modern interpretations of "The Tempest" often focus on themes of colonialism and imperialism, with Prospero's domination of the island and its inhabitants (Caliban and Ariel) reflecting European colonial practices. Postcolonial readings have further analyzed the dynamics of power, race, and resistance.

The Role of Caliban: Caliban, often considered one of Shakespeare's most complex characters, represents the island's native population. His character has been variously interpreted as a figure of natural man, a symbol of colonial oppression, and as embodying the darker aspects of human nature.

. . .

Music and Soundscape: "The Tempest" is notable for its extensive use of music and sound, which enhance the magical atmosphere of the island. The songs and sounds are integral to the storytelling, influencing the mood and advancing the plot.

Masque Elements: The play incorporates elements of the masque, a form of festive courtly entertainment that combines music, dance, and elaborate staging. This is most evident in the betrothal masque for Ferdinand and Miranda, underscoring the play's themes of harmony and social order.

Miranda's Innocence and Awakening: Miranda, Prospero's daughter, represents innocence and virtue. Her exposure to the shipwrecked courtiers and her love for Ferdinand symbolize the awakening of consciousness and the discovery of the other.

The Shipwreck as a Plot Device: The play begins with a shipwreck, orchestrated by Prospero's magic, which brings his enemies to the island. This event sets the stage for the themes of justice, redemption, and mercy that unfold.

Ariel and the Ethereal: Ariel, a spirit bound to serve Prospero, represents the ethereal and magical aspects of the world. His longing for freedom and his role in executing Prospero's plans highlight themes of servitude and liberation.

The Chess Game: The play ends with a chess game between Ferdinand and Miranda, symbolizing strategy, the complexities of human interaction, and the idea of life as a series of strategic moves.

"The Tempest" and Shakespeare's Retirement: The play is often seen as Shakespeare's farewell to the theater. Prospero's renunciation of his magical powers and his return to Milan are interpreted as Shakespeare's own retirement from the London stage.

. . .

Performance History and Adaptations: "The Tempest" has a rich performance history, from Restoration adaptations that added music and spectacle, to 20th and 21st-century productions that have explored its themes of power, colonialism, and the supernatural through various interpretive lenses.

Film and Operatic Adaptations: The play has inspired numerous film and operatic adaptations, showcasing its enduring appeal and flexibility. These adaptations have ranged from faithful renditions to creative reimaginings that transport the story to new settings and contexts.

The Play's Legacy: "The Tempest" has left a lasting legacy in literature and the arts, influencing countless works and continuing to be a source of study and artistic inspiration. Its exploration of the human condition, power dynamics, and the transformative power of forgiveness ensures its relevance across the ages.

ABOUT THE AUTHOR

Jeanette Vigon is a vibrant storyteller hailing from the sun-kissed beaches of California, where her Spanish heritage infuses her writing with a colorful zest for life. Born to Spanish immigrants who carried stories of their homeland across the ocean, Jeanette's childhood was rich with tales that sparked her imagination and sowed the seeds for her future in storytelling.

After completing her education with a focus on early childhood development, Jeanette dedicated herself to the noble profession of teaching. As a beloved primary school teacher, she spent years enlightening young minds in the classroom. Her magical ability to turn even the most mundane lesson into a memorable adventure earned her admiration from both her pupils and peers.

However, the call of the pen proved too strong for Jeanette to ignore. Diving headfirst into the world of literature, she transitioned from shaping minds with chalk to enchanting them with words as a full-time writer. Her intimate knowledge of children's learning styles, combined with her rich cultural roots, enables her to craft stories that are not only engaging but also educational.

Jeanette's writing is characterized by its empathy, humor, and a deep understanding of what captivates children's hearts and minds. Whether retelling a classic Shakespearean tale or penning an original story, her books are beloved for their ability to bridge cultural gaps and bring diverse experiences to the forefront of children's literature.

Now, with several acclaimed titles to her name, Jeanette continues to share her passion for enriching young lives through reading. When she's not lost in her latest manuscript, you can find her indulging in her love for travel, exploring new destinations, and collecting fresh inspirations for her next enchanting narrative.

It's hard for books to get noticed these days. Whether you liked this one or not, please consider writing a review, thanks!

Jeanette Vigon

Printed in Dunstable, United Kingdom